Mastering SAP Extended Warehouse Management (EWM): A Comprehensive Guide

Table of Contents

Chapter 1: Introduction to SAP Extended Warehouse Management

Welcome to Chapter 1 of "Mastering SAP Extended Warehouse Management (EWM): A Comprehensive Guide." In this chapter, we will provide you with an introduction to SAP Extended Warehouse Management (EWM), its key features and benefits, and an overview of its architecture and components. Let's get started!

1.1 Overview of SAP Extended Warehouse Management

SAP Extended Warehouse Management (EWM) is a powerful software solution that helps organizations efficiently manage their warehouse operations and inventory. It provides comprehensive functionality for all aspects of warehouse management, including inbound and outbound processes, internal warehouse processes, resource management, labor management, and more.

With SAP EWM, businesses can optimize their warehouse operations, improve inventory accuracy, enhance order fulfillment processes, and achieve higher levels of customer satisfaction. It offers advanced features such as task management, wave management, labor management, yard management, and integration with other SAP modules and third-party systems.

1.2 Key Features and Benefits of SAP Extended Warehouse Management

SAP EWM offers several key features and benefits that make it a preferred choice for warehouse management:

Advanced Warehouse Processes: SAP EWM supports a wide range of warehouse processes, including goods receipt, putaway, order fulfillment, shipping, stock transfers, replenishment, value-added services, and cross-docking. These processes can be customized to meet the specific needs of your business.

Task Management: EWM's task management functionality allows you to create, release, and manage tasks efficiently. It provides flexible strategies for task creation, wave management for order processing, task interleaving, sequencing, and confirmation.

Resource Management: EWM helps you optimize resource allocation and utilization in your warehouse. You can define work centers, workstations, and labor standards, and monitor resource availability in real-time. This feature enables effective capacity planning and resource optimization.

Yard Management: With SAP EWM's yard management capabilities, you can efficiently manage your yard operations, including gate and appointment management, yard movements, and status tracking. This integration streamlines the flow of goods between the warehouse and transportation.

Integration with Other SAP Modules: SAP EWM seamlessly integrates with other SAP modules, such as SAP ERP (Material Management and Sales and Distribution), SAP Transportation Management (TM), and SAP Global Trade Services (GTS). This integration ensures end-to-end visibility and streamlines processes across the supply chain.

1.3 EWM Architecture and Components

SAP EWM consists of various components that work together to provide a comprehensive warehouse management solution. The key components include:

Warehouse Structure: This component allows you to define and configure the physical structure of your warehouse, including warehouses, storage types, storage sections, and storage bins. You can also define bin types, handling units, and packaging materials.

Warehouse Process Types: EWM supports different warehouse process types, such as inbound processes, outbound processes, and internal warehouse processes. Each process type has specific functionalities and settings tailored to the process requirements.

Warehouse Task Management: This component is responsible for managing and executing warehouse tasks. It includes functionalities for task creation, release strategies, task confirmation, and completion. Task management ensures the efficient execution of warehouse operations.

Resource Management: The resource management component enables you to define work centers, workstations, labor standards, and manage resource availability. It helps optimize resource allocation, capacity planning, and monitors labor productivity.

Yard Management: This component allows you to manage your yard operations, including gate and appointment management, yard movements, and status tracking. It integrates with transportation management systems to ensure smooth coordination between the warehouse and transportation.

Reporting and Analytics: SAP EWM provides robust reporting and analytics capabilities. You can monitor key performance indicators (KPIs), track warehouse activities in real-time, and gain valuable insights into warehouse operations through various reporting tools and dashboards.

Now that you have a good understanding of the overview, features, and architecture of SAP Extended Warehouse Management (EWM), you are ready to dive deeper into the various aspects of EWM. In the next chapter, we will explore the setup and installation of SAP EWM.

Stay tuned for Chapter 2: Setting Up SAP EWM.

Chapter 2: Setting Up SAP Extended Warehouse Management

In Chapter 2, we will walk you through the process of setting up SAP Extended Warehouse Management (EWM). This chapter will cover the system landscape and technical requirements, preparing for the EWM implementation, installation and configuration of SAP EWM, and integration with SAP ERP and other modules. Let's get started!

2.1 System Landscape and Technical Requirements

Before setting up SAP EWM, it is crucial to understand the system landscape and ensure that you have the necessary technical infrastructure in place. Here are the key considerations:

Hardware Requirements: Assess your hardware infrastructure to ensure that it meets the recommended specifications for running SAP EWM effectively. This includes server capacity, memory, disk space, and network connectivity.

Software Requirements: Determine the software components required for SAP EWM, such as the operating system, database management system, and other prerequisite software. Ensure that you have the necessary licenses and installations for these components.

System Landscape Design: Plan the structure of your SAP landscape, including the production system, development system, and quality assurance system. Consider whether you will have a centralized or decentralized landscape, and ensure proper connectivity between the systems.

2.2 Preparing for the EWM Implementation

Successful implementation of SAP EWM requires careful planning and preparation. Consider the following steps:

Project Scope Definition: Clearly define the scope of your EWM implementation project. Identify the specific functionalities and processes you want to implement, and prioritize them based on business requirements.

Business Process Analysis: Analyze your existing warehouse management processes and identify areas for improvement. Understand your current challenges and pain points, and determine how SAP EWM can address them effectively.

Resource Allocation: Allocate the necessary resources for the EWM implementation, including project team members, subject matter experts, and technical resources. Ensure that all stakeholders are actively involved and committed to the project.

Data Preparation: Identify the data required for SAP EWM implementation, such as product master data, customer data, and vendor data. Cleanse and prepare the data to ensure its accuracy and consistency before the migration.

2.3 Installation and Configuration of SAP EWM

Once you have prepared the necessary infrastructure and completed the initial planning, you can proceed with the installation and configuration of SAP EWM. Follow these steps:

Installation of SAP EWM: Install the SAP EWM software on the designated server or servers according to the installation guide provided by SAP. Ensure that all prerequisites and dependencies are met before starting the installation process.

System Configuration: Configure the SAP EWM system to align with your warehouse management requirements. This includes defining the organizational structure, storage types, storage bins, and other master data elements. Configure settings related to warehouse processes, resource management, and labor management.

Integration with SAP ERP: Establish integration between SAP EWM and SAP ERP or other relevant SAP modules. Configure settings for data exchange, such as master data replication, stock synchronization, and transactional data flow.

Testing and Validation: Perform thorough testing and validation of the EWM system to ensure that it functions as expected. Conduct unit testing, integration testing, and user acceptance testing to verify the system's performance, accuracy, and compliance with business requirements.

2.4 Integration with Other SAP Modules

To leverage the full potential of SAP EWM, integrate it with other SAP modules. Consider the following integrations:

Integration with SAP ERP: Integrate EWM with SAP ERP modules such as Material Management (MM) and Sales and

Distribution (SD). This integration enables seamless data flow between the warehouse and other business processes, ensuring accurate inventory management and order fulfillment.

Integration with SAP Transportation Management (TM): Connect EWM with SAP TM to enable end-to-end visibility and control over warehouse and transportation operations. This integration streamlines transportation planning, execution, and tracking, ensuring efficient goods movement.

Integration with SAP Global Trade Services (GTS): If your organization deals with international trade and customs regulations, integrate EWM with SAP GTS. This integration facilitates compliance with trade laws, enables efficient customs documentation management, and ensures smooth cross-border movements.

Integration with Other SAP Solutions and Third-Party Systems: Explore additional integrations based on your specific business requirements. SAP EWM can be integrated with various SAP solutions, such as SAP Extended Supply Chain solutions, as well as third-party systems, enabling seamless data exchange and collaboration.

Congratulations! You have completed Chapter 2, which covered setting up SAP Extended Warehouse Management. In the next chapter, we will delve into the organizational structures in SAP EWM, including defining warehouses, storage types, storage bins, and product master data.

Stay tuned for Chapter 3: Organizational Structures in SAP EWM.

Chapter 3: Organizational Structures in SAP Extended Warehouse Management

In Chapter 3, we will focus on the organizational structures in SAP Extended Warehouse Management (EWM). These structures form the foundation of your warehouse setup and play a crucial role in defining the layout, storage, and management of your inventory. We will cover topics such as defining warehouses, storage types, storage sections, storage bins, and creating product master data. Let's get started!

3.1 Defining Warehouses

The first step in setting up your warehouse in SAP EWM is to define the physical warehouses in which your inventory will be stored. Follow these steps:

Access the SAP EWM system and navigate to the Warehouse Management IMG (Implementation Guide) by using transaction code SPRO.

Under the IMG structure, go to "Extended Warehouse Management" > "Master Data" > "Define Warehouse" to access the warehouse definition settings.

Create a new entry for each warehouse by specifying the warehouse number, name, and description. You can also define additional attributes such as the storage control indicator and warehouse category.

Save your settings. The warehouses are now defined in the system and can be used for further configuration.

3.2 Configuring Storage Types and Storage Sections

Storage types and storage sections define the different areas within your warehouse where products are stored. Follow these steps to configure storage types and sections:

In the Warehouse Management IMG, navigate to "Master Data" > "Define Storage Type" to access the storage type configuration settings.

Create storage types that reflect the different types of storage areas in your warehouse. Examples of storage types include bulk storage, picking area, staging area, and reserve storage.

Assign relevant indicators and attributes to each storage type, such as storage type category, picking indicator, storage behavior, and capacity check settings.

Save your settings. The storage types are now defined and can be used for further configuration.

If required, you can further divide storage types into storage sections. Storage sections allow for more granular control over the storage areas within a storage type. Repeat the steps above to define and configure storage sections within each storage type.

3.3 Defining Storage Bins

Storage bins represent the smallest units of storage within your warehouse. They define the physical locations where products are placed. Follow these steps to define storage bins:

In the Warehouse Management IMG, navigate to "Master Data" > "Define Storage Bin Structure" to access the storage bin configuration settings.

Define the structure of your storage bins by specifying the hierarchy of levels, such as aisle, rack, shelf, and bin number. This structure depends on the layout of your warehouse and the level of detail required for your inventory management.

Configure additional attributes for each storage bin level, such as dimensions, weight capacity, storage type assignment, and bin type.

Save your settings. The storage bin structure is now defined, and you can proceed with creating storage bins.

In the same IMG node, go to "Master Data" > "Create Storage Bin" to create storage bins within the defined structure. Enter the relevant details, such as storage bin number, storage type, and coordinates according to the defined structure.

Save your settings. Repeat this step to create storage bins for the entire warehouse.

3.4 Creating Product Master Data

Product master data is essential for accurate inventory management in SAP EWM. It includes information such as product descriptions, dimensions, weight, and packaging details. Follow these steps to create product master data:

Access the SAP EWM system and navigate to the Warehouse Management IMG.

Under the IMG structure, go to "Product Master Data" > "Material Master Data" to access the material master settings.

Create or update material master records for the products stored in your warehouse. Enter the relevant information, including material number, description, dimensions, weight, and packaging details.

Save your settings. The product master data is now created and can be used for further warehouse operations.

Congratulations! You have completed Chapter 3, which covered the organizational structures in SAP Extended Warehouse Management. In the next chapter, we will explore warehouse process types, including inbound processes such as goods receipt and putaway, outbound processes such as order fulfillment and shipping, and internal warehouse processes. Stay tuned for Chapter 4: Warehouse Process Types.

Chapter 4: Warehouse Process Types

In Chapter 4, we will delve into the various warehouse process types in SAP Extended Warehouse Management (EWM). These process types encompass a range of activities, including inbound processes for goods receipt and putaway, outbound processes for order fulfillment and shipping, as well as internal warehouse processes. Let's explore each process type in detail.

4.1 Inbound Processes

Inbound processes involve the receipt of goods into the warehouse and their subsequent placement in storage. The key steps in inbound processes are goods receipt and putaway. Here's an overview of each step:

4.1.1 Goods Receipt

Receive the goods from suppliers or production facilities.

Perform necessary checks, such as verifying the quantity, quality, and condition of the goods.

Create a goods receipt document in SAP EWM to capture the receipt of the goods. This document serves as a record of the received items and triggers subsequent warehouse processes.

Perform goods receipt posting, which updates inventory levels and triggers subsequent putaway processes.

4.1.2 Putaway

Determine the appropriate storage location for the received goods based on predefined putaway rules. These rules consider factors such as product characteristics, storage capacity, and proximity to the picking area.

Generate putaway tasks in SAP EWM to instruct warehouse personnel on the optimal storage bin for each item.

Execute the putaway tasks, ensuring that goods are placed in the designated storage bin.

Update inventory records to reflect the new storage location of the items.

4.2 Outbound Processes

Outbound processes involve the picking, packing, and shipping of goods to fulfill customer orders. The key steps in outbound processes are order fulfillment and shipping. Here's an overview of each step:

4.2.1 Order Fulfillment

Receive customer orders in SAP EWM.

Determine the availability of the ordered items in the warehouse.

Generate picking tasks based on predefined picking strategies, such as zone picking, batch picking, or wave picking. These tasks guide warehouse personnel on the retrieval of items from storage bins.

Execute the picking tasks, ensuring accurate retrieval of the required items.

Confirm the picked quantities and update inventory records accordingly.

4.2.2 Packing

Retrieve the picked items and proceed to the packing area.

Determine the appropriate packaging materials and methods based on order requirements, product characteristics, and shipping regulations.

Pack the items into the selected packaging materials, ensuring proper labeling and documentation.

Update inventory records to reflect the packed quantities.

4.2.3 Shipping

Prepare shipping documents, such as delivery notes and shipping labels.

Determine the most suitable shipping method and carrier for the order.

Arrange for transportation and coordinate with the carrier for pick-up or delivery.

Update the status of the order in SAP EWM to reflect its readiness for shipping.

Generate shipping documents and labels to accompany the shipment.

Hand over the goods to the carrier for transportation to the customer.

4.3 Internal Warehouse Processes

Internal warehouse processes involve the movement of goods within the warehouse, such as stock transfers and replenishment. Here's an overview of each process:

4.3.1 Stock Transfers

Initiate a stock transfer request to move goods from one storage bin to another within the same warehouse or across different warehouses.

Generate stock transfer tasks in SAP EWM to guide warehouse personnel on the physical movement of goods.

Execute the stock transfer tasks, ensuring accurate transfer of the items.

Update inventory records to reflect the new storage location of the transferred goods.

4.3.2 Replenishment

Monitor inventory levels to identify low-stock situations.

Generate replenishment tasks to move goods from reserve storage areas to picking areas.

Execute the replenishment tasks to ensure that picking areas have sufficient stock to fulfill customer orders.

Update inventory records to reflect the replenished quantities.

Congratulations! You have completed Chapter 4, which covered the various warehouse process types in SAP Extended Warehouse Management. In the next chapter, we will dive into warehouse task management, including task creation, release strategies, task confirmation, and completion. Stay tuned for Chapter 5: Warehouse Task Management.

Chapter 5: Warehouse Task Management

In Chapter 5, we will explore the important aspect of warehouse task management in SAP Extended Warehouse Management (EWM). Effective task management is crucial for optimizing warehouse operations and ensuring timely and accurate execution of tasks. We will cover topics such as task creation, release strategies, task confirmation, and completion. Let's dive in!

5.1 Task Creation

Task creation involves generating specific instructions for warehouse personnel to perform various activities within the warehouse. These activities can include picking, putaway, replenishment, packing, and more. Here's an overview of the task creation process:

Identify the activities that need to be performed within the warehouse, such as picking orders or replenishing stock.

Determine the criteria for task creation, such as order priority, item availability, or resource availability.

Use the task creation functionality in SAP EWM to generate tasks based on the predefined criteria. This functionality considers factors like item location, storage bin capacity, and proximity to the picking area.

Assign the generated tasks to the appropriate resources, such as forklift operators or pickers.

Provide the necessary details and instructions within the task, including item information, quantity to be picked, destination storage bin, and any special handling requirements.

5.2 Task Release Strategies

Task release strategies determine the conditions under which tasks are released for execution. By defining release strategies, you can automate the task release process and ensure that tasks are assigned to the right resources at the right time. Here's an overview of the task release strategy configuration:

Define the criteria for releasing tasks based on factors such as workload, resource availability, or order priorities.

Configure the release strategies in SAP EWM, specifying the conditions that must be met for tasks to be released.

Assign the release strategies to specific warehouses, storage types, or other relevant parameters.

SAP EWM will automatically evaluate the release criteria against the current warehouse conditions, triggering the release of tasks that meet the defined criteria.

5.3 Task Confirmation

Task confirmation involves validating that a task has been successfully completed. It enables accurate tracking of task progress and provides real-time updates on warehouse operations. Here's an overview of the task confirmation process:

Warehouse personnel perform the assigned task, such as picking items or transferring stock.

After completing the task, the personnel confirm the task in SAP EWM. This can be done through various methods, such as barcode scanning, mobile devices, or manual entry.

During task confirmation, the system verifies the accuracy of the completed task, ensuring that the correct quantities have been picked or transferred.

Warehouse personnel can provide additional information during task confirmation, such as the reason for any discrepancies or any required follow-up actions.

The task confirmation updates the task status in SAP EWM, reflecting the task's completion and triggering subsequent processes, such as inventory updates or order status updates.

5.4 Task Completion

Task completion involves finalizing the task and updating the relevant data in SAP EWM. It ensures accurate and up-to-date information about warehouse operations. Here's an overview of the task completion process:

After task confirmation, SAP EWM performs any necessary updates to inventory quantities, storage bin statuses, or order statuses.

The system updates the task status as completed, indicating that the task has been successfully executed.

Task completion triggers subsequent processes, such as order status updates, replenishment triggers, or stock availability notifications.

The completed task data is available for reporting and analysis, providing insights into warehouse performance, resource utilization, and overall efficiency.

Congratulations! You have completed Chapter 5, which covered warehouse task management in SAP Extended Warehouse Management. In the next chapter, we will explore resource management, including the configuration of resources, capacity planning, and resource optimization. Stay tuned for Chapter 6: Resource Management.

Chapter 6: Resource Management

In Chapter 6, we will delve into resource management in SAP Extended Warehouse Management (EWM). Efficient resource management is vital for optimizing warehouse operations and ensuring the availability of the necessary resources to perform tasks. We will cover topics such as the configuration of resources (work centers and workstations), capacity planning, resource optimization, and integration with labor management and time recording. Let's get started!

6.1 Configuring Resources

Configuring resources involves defining the work centers and workstations within your warehouse. These resources represent the physical locations where warehouse tasks are performed. Here's an overview of the resource configuration process:

Identify the work centers and workstations within your warehouse where tasks are executed. Work centers can be areas such as picking zones, packing stations, or shipping docks.

Access the Warehouse Management IMG in SAP EWM.

Navigate to "Resource Management" > "Define Resource" to access the resource configuration settings.

Create resource master data for each work center or workstation, specifying details such as the resource number, description, capacity, and attributes.

Assign the resource to the corresponding work center or workstation. This assignment links the resource to the physical location within the warehouse.

Configure additional settings for the resource, such as operating times, availability, and any special requirements or restrictions.

Save your settings. The resources are now defined in the system and can be utilized for task assignments and capacity planning.

6.2 Capacity Planning and Resource Optimization

Capacity planning involves estimating the workload and determining the capacity required to execute warehouse tasks efficiently. Resource optimization ensures that resources are utilized effectively to meet the demands of warehouse operations. Here's an overview of capacity planning and resource optimization:

Analyze historical data, such as task volumes, processing times, and peak periods, to understand the workload patterns in your warehouse.

Use the capacity planning functionality in SAP EWM to estimate the resource capacity required to meet the workload demands. This estimation considers factors such as task types, task durations, and resource availability.

Evaluate the resource capacity against the estimated workload and identify any potential bottlenecks or imbalances.

Optimize resource utilization by adjusting task assignments, redistributing workloads, or reallocating resources based on workload fluctuations.

Monitor resource utilization and performance metrics, such as resource efficiency, utilization rates, and productivity.

Continuously review and refine capacity planning and resource optimization strategies based on changing business needs and operational requirements.

6.3 Integration with Labor Management and Time Recording

Integrating resource management with labor management and time recording provides comprehensive visibility and control over workforce activities within the warehouse. Here's an overview of the integration process:

Configure integration settings between resource management, labor management, and time recording modules in SAP EWM.

Define labor standards and work measurement methods to establish benchmarks for task durations and resource productivity.

Capture employee time and attendance data using time recording methods such as clock-in/out terminals or mobile devices.

Integrate labor data with resource management to track actual resource utilization, compare it with planned capacity, and identify any variances.

Analyze labor data to measure productivity, identify areas for improvement, and support performance management initiatives.

Use labor data in capacity planning and resource optimization processes to refine resource allocation and workload balancing strategies.

Leverage labor management and time recording insights for reporting and analytics to support decision-making and continuous improvement efforts.

Congratulations! You have completed Chapter 6, which covered resource management in SAP Extended Warehouse Management. In the next chapter, we will explore labor management, including the definition of labor standards, tracking and analyzing labor productivity, incentive and performance management, as well as reporting and analytics for labor management. Stay tuned for Chapter 7: Labor Management.

Chapter 7: Labor Management

In Chapter 7, we will dive into labor management in SAP Extended Warehouse Management (EWM). Effective labor management ensures optimal workforce productivity, accurate tracking of labor activities, and supports performance management initiatives within the warehouse. We will cover topics such as the definition of labor standards, tracking and analyzing labor productivity, incentive and performance management, as well as reporting and analytics for labor management. Let's get started!

7.1 Definition of Labor Standards

Labor standards provide a baseline for measuring and evaluating the performance of warehouse labor activities. They define the expected time and effort required to complete specific tasks or operations. Here's an overview of the labor standards definition process:

Analyze historical data and conduct time studies to determine the average time taken to perform various warehouse tasks accurately.

Define labor standards for each task or operation in terms of time required, taking into account factors such as task complexity, skill level, and equipment used.

Consider additional factors that may impact labor standards, such as variations in product size, weight, or pick density.

Configure labor standard settings in SAP EWM, associating each task or operation with the corresponding labor standard.

Regularly review and update labor standards based on actual performance data and continuous improvement initiatives.

7.2 Tracking and Analyzing Labor Productivity

Tracking and analyzing labor productivity is essential for measuring performance, identifying areas for improvement, and ensuring optimal resource utilization within the warehouse. Here's an overview of the process:

Capture labor data, including start and end times for each task or operation, using methods such as time recording terminals, mobile devices, or manual entry.

Integrate labor data with task management and resource management modules in SAP EWM to associate labor activities with specific tasks and resources.

Calculate labor productivity metrics, such as units picked per hour, tasks completed per shift, or order fulfillment rates, based on the captured data.

Analyze labor productivity metrics to identify trends, patterns, and performance gaps. Compare actual performance against labor standards and benchmarks.

Identify areas for improvement, such as process bottlenecks, training needs, or resource allocation adjustments based on labor productivity analysis.

Leverage reporting and analytics tools in SAP EWM to generate labor productivity reports and dashboards for monitoring and decision-making purposes.

7.3 Incentive and Performance Management

Incentive and performance management programs encourage and reward exceptional performance, motivating warehouse personnel to achieve high productivity levels. Here's an overview of incentive and performance management in SAP EWM:

Define performance metrics and targets aligned with warehouse goals and labor standards. These metrics can include productivity rates, accuracy levels, or order turnaround times.

Establish incentive programs that provide rewards, such as monetary bonuses, recognition, or additional benefits, for employees who meet or exceed performance targets.

Configure incentive rules and calculations in SAP EWM, taking into account factors such as task complexity, individual performance, or team-based achievements.

Monitor performance metrics and calculate incentive payouts based on actual performance data captured in SAP EWM.

Communicate performance results, provide feedback, and recognize top performers to reinforce a culture of excellence and continuous improvement.

7.4 Reporting and Analytics for Labor Management

Reporting and analytics tools in SAP EWM provide valuable insights into labor management, enabling data-driven decision-making and continuous improvement. Here's an overview of reporting and analytics capabilities:

Leverage predefined reports and dashboards in SAP EWM to monitor labor-related KPIs, such as productivity rates, labor costs, or overtime usage.

Customize reports and dashboards to suit specific business requirements and stakeholders' needs.

Use advanced analytics features, such as data visualization tools or predictive analytics, to gain deeper insights into labor performance, identify trends, or forecast resource requirements.

Share labor management reports and analytics with relevant stakeholders, such as warehouse managers, supervisors, or HR personnel, to support performance evaluation, resource planning, and decision-making processes.

Congratulations! You have completed Chapter 7, which covered labor management in SAP Extended Warehouse Management. In the next chapter, we will explore yard management, including yard setup and configuration, gate and appointment management, yard movements, and integration with transportation management. Stay tuned for Chapter 8: Yard Management.

Chapter 8: Yard Management

In Chapter 8, we will explore yard management in SAP Extended Warehouse Management (EWM). Yard management focuses on efficiently managing the flow of goods and vehicles within the warehouse yard area. We will cover topics such as yard setup and configuration, gate and appointment management, yard movements, and integration with transportation management. Let's dive in!

8.1 Yard Setup and Configuration

The setup and configuration of the yard in SAP EWM involve defining the physical layout and characteristics of the yard area. Here's an overview of the yard setup process:

Analyze the layout of your warehouse yard area and determine the zones, lanes, and parking spots for various types of vehicles, such as trucks or trailers.

Access the Warehouse Management IMG in SAP EWM.

Navigate to "Yard Management" > "Define Yard Areas" to access the yard configuration settings.

Define the yard areas based on the physical layout, assigning names, descriptions, and other relevant attributes.

Configure additional settings for the yard areas, such as capacity, utilization rules, or restrictions for certain vehicle types.

Save your settings. The yard areas are now defined in the system and ready for further configuration.

8.2 Gate and Appointment Management

Gate and appointment management in yard management involve coordinating the entry and exit of vehicles into the warehouse yard area. Here's an overview of the gate and appointment management process:

Define the gates in SAP EWM, specifying the entry and exit points of the warehouse yard area.

Configure gate settings, such as gate types, gate control methods (manual or automated), and security requirements.

Establish appointment management procedures to schedule and manage the arrival and departure of vehicles in the yard.

Enable appointment creation and booking functionalities in SAP EWM, allowing carriers or transporters to request specific time slots for vehicle arrivals.

Implement gate control processes to validate appointments, verify vehicle information, and grant access to authorized vehicles.

Monitor and track the status of vehicles at the gate, ensuring smooth and efficient vehicle flow within the yard area.

8.3 Yard Movements

Yard movements involve the tracking and coordination of vehicle movements within the warehouse yard area. Here's an overview of the yard movement process:

Implement vehicle identification methods, such as RFID tags or barcode scanning, to track and identify vehicles within the yard.

Enable yard movement functionalities in SAP EWM to record and manage vehicle movements, including entry, parking, loading/unloading, and departure.

Assign parking spots or parking zones to incoming vehicles based on availability, vehicle types, or specific requirements.

Capture vehicle-related information, such as arrival and departure timestamps, parking durations, and movement details, in SAP EWM.

Enable real-time visibility and tracking of vehicle movements through the use of yard management dashboards, reports, or integration with tracking technologies.

Automate yard movements where possible, leveraging technologies such as automated guided vehicles (AGVs) or yard management systems (YMS) to optimize vehicle routing and reduce manual efforts.

8.4 Integration with Transportation Management

Integration between yard management and transportation management systems ensures seamless coordination between warehouse yard operations and transportation processes. Here's an overview of the integration process:

Establish integration settings between SAP EWM and SAP Transportation Management (TM) modules.

Enable data exchange between the systems, such as sharing vehicle-related information, appointment data, or delivery schedules.

Align yard management processes with transportation planning and execution processes, ensuring consistency in vehicle scheduling, loading/unloading activities, and transportation resources.

Leverage integration capabilities to provide real-time updates on yard activities, vehicle statuses, or any changes in transportation plans.

Enable communication channels between yard management personnel, transportation planners, and carriers to facilitate information exchange and collaboration.

Congratulations! You have completed Chapter 8, which covered yard management in SAP Extended Warehouse Management. In the next chapter, we will explore reporting and analytics in SAP EWM, including the available reporting tools, key performance indicators (KPIs), and data analysis techniques. Stay tuned for Chapter 9: Reporting and Analytics.

Chapter 9: Reporting and Analytics

In Chapter 9, we will explore reporting and analytics in SAP Extended Warehouse Management (EWM). Reporting and analytics provide valuable insights into warehouse operations, performance, and key metrics, enabling data-driven decision-making and continuous improvement. We will cover topics such as available reporting tools, key performance indicators (KPIs), data analysis techniques, and visualization methods. Let's dive in!

9.1 Reporting Tools in SAP EWM

SAP EWM offers a range of reporting tools to extract, analyze, and visualize data related to warehouse operations. These tools enable you to generate reports and dashboards that provide insights into various aspects of your warehouse. Here are some of the reporting tools available:

Standard Reports: SAP EWM provides a set of standard reports that cover key warehouse processes such as inbound processes, outbound processes, stock overview, and resource utilization. These reports offer predefined layouts and can be customized to meet specific reporting requirements.

Report Writer: The Report Writer tool in SAP EWM allows you to create customized reports by selecting the desired data fields, defining calculations, and specifying filters and sorting options. It provides flexibility in designing reports tailored to your specific needs.

Query Designer: The Query Designer tool enables you to create ad-hoc queries and reports using a drag-and-drop interface. It allows you to select data sources, define joins and conditions, and design the output layout. Query Designer is a powerful tool for on-the-fly reporting and analysis.

Business Intelligence (BI) Tools: SAP EWM can be integrated with SAP Business Intelligence (BI) tools, such as SAP BusinessObjects or SAP Analytics Cloud. These tools offer advanced reporting and analytics capabilities, including interactive dashboards, data visualization, and predictive analytics.

9.2 Key Performance Indicators (KPIs)

Key performance indicators (KPIs) provide a quantifiable measure of warehouse performance and help evaluate the success of warehouse operations. SAP EWM offers a range of predefined KPIs that can be used to monitor and assess warehouse performance. Some common KPIs in EWM include:

Order Fulfillment Rate: Measures the percentage of customer orders that are successfully fulfilled within a specified time frame.

Inventory Accuracy: Measures the accuracy of inventory records by comparing the actual physical stock with the recorded stock in the system.

On-Time Delivery: Measures the percentage of orders that are delivered to customers on or before the promised delivery date.

Resource Utilization: Measures the efficiency of resource utilization, such as labor productivity, equipment usage, or warehouse space utilization.

Order Cycle Time: Measures the average time taken to process an order from receipt to delivery.

Picking Accuracy: Measures the accuracy of the picking process by comparing the picked quantities with the ordered quantities.

These KPIs can be monitored using the reporting tools available in SAP EWM, enabling you to track performance, identify areas for improvement, and make data-driven decisions.

9.3 Data Analysis Techniques

In addition to standard reports and predefined KPIs, SAP EWM provides various data analysis techniques to extract meaningful insights from warehouse data. Here are some commonly used data analysis techniques in EWM:

Data Segmentation: Segmenting warehouse data based on specific criteria allows you to analyze subsets of data and identify patterns or trends. For example, you can segment data by product categories, customer segments, or time periods.

Trend Analysis: Analyzing historical data helps identify trends over time, such as seasonality, demand patterns, or performance trends. Trend analysis enables proactive decision-making and resource planning.

Comparative Analysis: Comparing performance data across different warehouse locations, time periods, or product categories helps identify best practices, performance variations, or areas for improvement. Comparative analysis allows benchmarking and performance evaluation.

Root Cause Analysis: When investigating performance issues or deviations, conducting root cause analysis helps identify the underlying factors contributing to the problem. By analyzing data at a granular level, you can pinpoint the root causes of inefficiencies or errors.

Predictive Analytics: Leveraging advanced analytics techniques, such as predictive modeling or machine learning algorithms, allows you to forecast future warehouse performance, anticipate demand fluctuations, or predict resource requirements.

9.4 Visualization Methods

Visualizing data in a clear and intuitive manner enhances data interpretation and facilitates better understanding of warehouse performance. SAP EWM provides visualization methods to present data in meaningful formats. Some common visualization methods include:

Charts and Graphs: Bar charts, line charts, pie charts, and scatter plots can effectively present data trends, comparisons, and distributions. These visual representations make it easier to identify patterns or anomalies in warehouse data.

Dashboards: Interactive dashboards provide a consolidated view of key metrics, KPIs, and performance indicators. They allow users to drill down into specific areas, filter data, and gain real-time visibility into warehouse operations.

Heat Maps: Heat maps use color gradients to represent data density or variations. They are useful for visualizing data related to inventory levels, order volumes, or resource utilization across different warehouse zones or time periods.

Geographic Maps: Geographic maps provide a spatial view of warehouse operations, showing the locations of warehouses, customers, or transportation routes. They are helpful for visualizing distribution networks, identifying regional performance variations, or optimizing transportation routes.

By leveraging these visualization methods, you can present complex warehouse data in a concise and understandable manner, facilitating effective decision-making and communication.

Congratulations! You have completed Chapter 9, which covered reporting and analytics in SAP Extended Warehouse Management. You have gained insights into the available reporting tools, key performance indicators (KPIs), data analysis techniques, and visualization methods. In the next chapter, we will explore advanced topics in SAP EWM, including integration with other SAP modules and emerging trends in warehouse management. Stay tuned for Chapter 10: Advanced Topics in SAP EWM.

Chapter 10: Advanced Topics in SAP EWM

In Chapter 10, we will delve into advanced topics in SAP Extended Warehouse Management (EWM). These topics include integration with other SAP modules, emerging trends in warehouse management, and additional features and functionalities. Let's explore these advanced topics:

10.1 Integration with Other SAP Modules

SAP EWM can be integrated with various other SAP modules to streamline and optimize end-to-end business processes. Here are some key integration points:

Integration with SAP ERP: Integration with SAP ERP modules such as Materials Management (MM) and Sales and Distribution (SD) ensures seamless data exchange between warehouse operations and other business functions. This integration enables efficient inventory management, order processing, and financial accounting.

Integration with SAP Transportation Management (TM): Integrating EWM with SAP TM allows for comprehensive control and visibility over warehouse and transportation operations. It facilitates efficient planning, execution, and tracking of goods movement from the warehouse to the customer, optimizing transportation routes and reducing costs.

Integration with SAP Global Trade Services (GTS): If your organization deals with international trade and compliance, integrating EWM with SAP GTS enables efficient management of customs regulations, trade documentation, and compliance checks. This integration ensures smooth cross-border movements and adherence to global trade laws.

Integration with SAP Extended Supply Chain Solutions: SAP EWM can be integrated with other solutions within the SAP Extended Supply Chain suite, such as SAP Advanced Planning and Optimization (APO), SAP Integrated Business Planning (IBP), and SAP Demand-Driven Replenishment (DDR). These integrations enhance end-to-end supply chain visibility and enable optimized planning and execution processes.

10.2 Emerging Trends in Warehouse Management

Warehouse management is constantly evolving to meet the changing demands of modern supply chains. Here are some emerging trends in warehouse management:

Automation and Robotics: The adoption of automation technologies, such as automated guided vehicles (AGVs), robotic process automation (RPA), and robotic picking systems, improves efficiency, accuracy, and scalability in warehouse operations.

Internet of Things (IoT) and Sensor Integration: Connecting devices and equipment within the warehouse through IoT and sensor integration enables real-time monitoring, data collection, and predictive analytics. This enhances visibility, asset tracking, and proactive maintenance.

Artificial Intelligence (AI) and Machine Learning (ML): AI and ML algorithms can analyze large volumes of data, identify patterns, and make intelligent predictions. These technologies can be applied in areas such as demand forecasting, route optimization, inventory management, and predictive maintenance.

Augmented Reality (AR) and Wearable Devices: AR technology, coupled with wearable devices, provides hands-free guidance, visual instructions, and real-time data display to warehouse operators, improving productivity, accuracy, and training efficiency.

10.3 Additional Features and Functionalities

SAP EWM offers additional features and functionalities to enhance warehouse management processes. Here are a few notable features:

Wave Management: Wave management allows for the grouping and sequential processing of warehouse tasks based on predefined criteria, optimizing resource utilization and order fulfillment efficiency.

Cross-Docking: Cross-docking enables the direct transfer of goods from the inbound dock to the outbound dock without intermediate putaway or storage. This reduces handling and storage costs and expedites order fulfillment.

Slotting and Replenishment Strategies: Slotting strategies determine the optimal placement of products within the warehouse based on factors such as demand, product characteristics, and storage capacity. Replenishment strategies automate the replenishment of picking locations based on predefined rules.

Returns Management: SAP EWM provides functionalities to manage and process product returns efficiently, including return order creation, return storage, inspection, and disposition.

Value-Added Services (VAS): SAP EWM supports value-added services such as kitting, assembly, labeling, and customization. These services enhance product value and customer satisfaction.

By leveraging these advanced features, staying abreast of emerging trends, and integrating SAP EWM with other modules, you can optimize warehouse management processes and stay competitive in the ever-evolving supply chain landscape.

Congratulations! You have completed Chapter 10, which covered advanced topics in SAP Extended Warehouse Management. You have gained insights into integration with other SAP modules, emerging trends in warehouse management, and additional features and functionalities. You now have a solid foundation to optimize your warehouse operations using SAP EWM. Best of luck on your journey of utilizing this powerful solution!

www.ingramcontent.com/pod-product-compliance
Lightning Source LLC
LaVergne TN
LVHW051618050326
832903LV00033B/4556